Recipes by
Lena Cara

Photos by
Rose Aloi Photography

VEGAN CHRISTMAS COOKBOOK

Christmas Classics With a Vegan Twist

CONTENTS

APPETIZERS

Antipasto Stocking..........................9

Pastry Wreath..........................11

Tomato & Pesto Bruscetta......................12

Roast Capsicum Cob Loaf Dip.................15

Stuffed Mushrooms...................................16

ENTREE

Gnocchi Bake................................. 21

Eggplant Meatballs............................22

Pea & Asparagus Risotto..........................25

Leak & Potato Soup............................26

Tomato & Peas Arancini............................28

MAINS

Pumpkin Roast...32

Tofu & Vegie Skewers..............................35

Sweet Potato Wellington...........................36

Root Vegetable Mini Pot Pies....................39

Mexican Baked Peppers............................40

SIDES

Cucumber & Tomato Salad......................44

Lemon & Herb Roast Potatoes.................47

Mashed Potato......................................48

Rocket, Pear & Walnut Salad...................51

Couscous Salad....................................52

DESSERTS

Choc. Coconut Rum Balls........................56

Choc. Hazelnut Christmas Tree...............59

Shortbread Cookies..............................60

Chocolate Bundt Cake...........................63

Cookies & Cream Truffles........................64

DRINKS

Coconut Hot Chocolate............................69

Vegan Eggnog..70

Gingerbread Hot Chocolate......................72

Pink Sangria...75

Cranberry & Lime Sparkler.......................76

INTRODUCTION

I first thought about creating this book after I moved out of home. I come from a very traditional Italian family, many of whom found it odd that I'd become vegetarian when I turned sixteen. When my younger sister followed in my footsteps several years later, then switched to a plant-based lifestyle a few years after that, my family was gobsmacked. Food like cheese, milk, cold-cuts and meat are huge staples in the Italian diet. It took a lot of convincing that when eating properly and making sure you were getting the right vitamins, minerals and protein in your diet, a vegan or plant-based diet was quite sustainable.

My sister loves cooking and before moving out, I'd be eating whatever she cooked. Through her, I became accustomed to the taste of soy milk, coconut yoghurt and a range of other soy and vegan alternatives. When I moved out, I found myself putting only vegan products in my shopping basket and avoiding foods like cow's milk, cheeses, butter and eggs. We live in a world that has so many more options than it did when I first became vegetarian over a decade ago. Being vegetarian back then usually meant that I could only order salads when I went to restaurants. Sometimes, if the kitchens were nice, they'd whip up a nice omelette with cheese. Nowadays, most restaurants have a range of vegan alternatives.

In this cookbook are several of my favourite recipes that my family has enjoyed (I only told them they were vegan after asking for their honest feedback about the dish). Whether you're vegan, looking to shift to a more vegan or plant-based diet or simply a flexitarian, this book is for you. Within these pages are a range of vegan recipes inspired by traditional Christmas dishes for you to cook and enjoy with your family and friends over the festive period. I hope you use and enjoy them as much as my family and I do.

Merry Christmas!

Lena Cardone

APPETIZERS

ANTIPASTO STOCKING

PREPARATION: 10 minutes   **BAKE:** 30 minutes   **SERVES:** 8

INGREDIENTS

2 sheets vegan puff
pastry, semi-thawed
½ cup sun-dried
tomatoes, coarsely
chopped
½ cup char grilled red
peppers, coarsely
chopped
½ cup Kalamata olives,
pitted and sliced
½ cup vegan feta,
crumbled
¼ cup pesto
1 tbsp soy milk

METHOD

Preheat the oven to 350°F (180°C).

Cut the puff pastry sheets into identical stocking shape (see photo on left for example).

In a medium-sized bowl, mix the semi-dried tomatoes, red peppers, olives and crumbed vegan feta.

Add the semi-dried tomato mixture to the top of one puff pastry sheet.

Slice straight lines across the second puff pastry sheet, leaving at least 1/2 inch (1.5cms) from the edge.

Place the second puff pastry sheet over the top of the first one and press the edges to enclose the pastry. Brush the top with soy milk.

Bake in the oven for 25-30 minutes, until pastry is golden brown.

Serve warm.

9

PASTRY WREATH

PREPARATION: 30 minutes   **BAKE:** 50 minutes   **SERVES:** 8

INGREDIENTS

¼ butternut pumpkin, cubed

½ red onion, thickly sliced

2 tbsp olive oil

½ tsp salt

¼ tsp black pepper

½ tsp oregano

¼ tsp onion powder

¼ tsp garlic powder

2 cups baby spinach

1 sheet vegan puff pastry, thawed

METHOD

Preheat the oven to 350°F (180°C). Lightly grease an oven tray and line it with baking paper.

To the oven tray, add the pumpkin, onion, olive oil, salt, pepper, oregano, onion powder and garlic powder and mix to coat well. Bake for 20 minutes, stirring halfway, until pumpkin is tender.

Add spinach to a small saucepan without water to wilt, stirring occasionally. The spinach will release its water and help the spinach cook.

Cut the pastry into a large circle (you can use a round plate to help). Take a pointed knife and carve a line from the centre of the pastry to halfway to the edge of the pastry. Repeat until you have 8 identical cuts from the centre of the pastry to halfway to the pastry edge.

Add spinach, pumpkin and pine nuts to the pastry and fold the centre of pastry flap up and over the pumpkin mixture, pressing down on edge to secure pastry ends. Bake for 25 minutes, until pastry is golden and serve.

TOMATO & PESTO BRUSCETTA

PREPARATION: 20 minutes   **BAKE:** 10 minutes   **SERVES:** 8

INGREDIENTS

6 tomatoes, cubed
1 red onion, coarsely chopped
¼ cup Extra Virgin olive oil
1 tsp oregano
1 tsp salt
¼ cup fresh basil, chipped
1 large Italian ciabatta or French baguette, cut into thick slices

Pesto
½ cups basil
½ cup baby spinach
¼ cup pine nuts or cashews
¼ cup olive oil
2 cloves garlic
salt & pepper (to taste)

METHOD

Preheat the oven to 350°F (180°C).

In a food processor, blend the basil, baby spinach, nuts, olive oil, salt and pepper until smooth.

In a mixing bowl, add the cubed tomatoes, onion, olive oil, oregano and salt. Toss to combine.

Toast the slices of bread on a lined baking tray for 10 minutes, then place on a serving platter.

Spread a thin layer of pesto to the top of each bread slice, then top with a spoonful of tomato mixture.

Garnish with chopped basil and extra dollops of pesto.

ROAST PEPPERS COB LOAF DIP

PREPARATION: 20 minutes   **BAKE:** 15 minutes   **COOK:** 5 minutes   **SERVES:** 8

INGREDIENTS

1 round loaf of bread
2 tbsp olive oil
1 brown onion, chopped
thinly
2 cups cashews, soaked
overnight or for a
minimum of 2 hours in
hot water
3-4 roasted red peppers
½ cup almond milk
1 small red chilli, seeds
removed
2 cloves garlic, minced
⅓ cup tahini
1 tsp smoked paprika
1 tsp salt
pinch of black pepper
2-3 tbsp water

METHOD

Preheat the oven to 390°F (200°C).

Slice off the top of the bread loaf and carefully pull out chunks of bread, making sure to not get too close to the crust edges.

Line bread on an oven tray lined with baking paper and bake for 10-15 minutes, until lightly toasted.

Heat olive oil in a small saucepan and sauté the onion until caramelised.

Add onion to a blender with cashews, roasted peppers, almond milk, chilli, garlic, tahini, paprika, salt, pepper and water. Blend for 30 seconds or so, until ingredients are well combined but not smooth.

Spoon into the hollow bread and serve with toasted chunks of bread on the side, warm.

STUFFED MUSHROOMS

PREPARATION: 30 minutes   **BAKE:** 40 minutes   **SERVES:** 4

INGREDIENTS

8 portobello flat
mushrooms, washed
and stems removed
1 cup plain breadcrumbs
1 clove garlic, crushed
¼ cup shopped parsley
1 tsp salt
½ tsp black pepper
¼ cup nutritional yeast
¼ cup vegan butter
1 cup vegan mozzarella

METHOD

Preheat the oven to 390°F (200°C).

Line an oven tray with baking paper and place mushrooms top up. Place into the oven for 10 minutes, then flip upside down and bake for a further 10 minutes.

Pour breadcrumbs into a medium-sized mixing bowl and add garlic, parsley, salt, pepper and nutritional yeast. Mix well.

Take mushrooms out and add ½ teaspoon of vegan butter to the centre of each upside down mushroom. Add a heaped teaspoon of breadcrumbs to each mushroom.

Top with vegan mozzarella and return tray to the oven. Bake for 15-20 minutes, until mozzarella begins to golden.

Serve warm.

ENTREE

GNOCCHI BAKE

PREPARATION: 25 minutes   **BAKE:** 40 minutes   **COOK:** 22 minutes   **SERVES:** 6

INGREDIENTS

500g vegan gnocchi
700ml Italian passata
sauce
½ red onion, cubed
2 cloves garlic, crushed
½ tsp sugar
1 tsp salt
¼ cup nutritional yeast
200g vegan mozzarella

METHOD

Preheat the oven to 350°F (180°C).

In a medium-sized saucepan, sauté onion and garlic for 1-2 minutes, until translucent. Add tomato passata. Simmer for 20 minutes and remove from heat.

While the pasta sauce cooks, in another saucepan, bring 1 litre of salted water to the oil and cook the gnocchi (check instructions on how to cook.)

Drain gnocchi and place into a deep oven dish. Add pasta sauce, nutritional yeast and half the mozzarella. Mix thoroughly.

Sprinkle the remaining mozzarella on top. Add aluminium foil and bake for 15 minutes.

Remove aluminium and bake for a further 25 minutes, until the top of mozzarella is golden.

EGGPLANT MEATBALLS

PREPARATION: 50 minutes   **COOK:** 20 minutes   **SERVES:** 8

INGREDIENTS

2 eggplants (aubergine), cubed
2 tbsp salt
2 tbsp ground flaxseed
6 tbsp water
1 garlic clove, minced
¾ cup parsley, chopped
1 white onion, diced
1½ cups breadcrumbs
1 cup vegan mozzarella
750ml vegetable or canola oil

METHOD

Take a colander and place the eggplants inside. Add the salt and set aside for 20-30 minutes.

While you wait, add the ground flaxseed and water and mix well. Set aside for 5-10 minutes, until thickened.

Take the eggplants and squeeze out the excess water. Place them in a food processor with the garlic, parsley, onion, breadcrumbs, flaxseed mixture and vegan mozzarella and process until all ingredients have been combined and there are no large chunks.

Scoop up a heaped spoonful of the eggplant mixture and, using your hands, mould it into a ball. Repeat until there is no mixture left.

In a medium-sized saucepan, add oil. Heat to cooking temperature. To check this, add a pinch of breadcrumbs to oil. If it reacts, you know it's ready for frying.

Fry the eggplant balls for 5-7 minutes, until they are golden. Repeat this process until all eggplants have been cooked.

TIP: Serve with spiced coconut dip, sweet chilli sauce or tomato ketchup.

PEA & ASPARAGUS RISOTTO

PREPARATION: 10 minutes   **COOK:** 40 minutes   **SERVES:** 6

INGREDIENTS

2 litres vegetable stock
1 tbsp olive oil
1 onion, finely chopped
1 garlic clove, minced
3 cup frozen peas,
thawed
3 cup asparagus, cut into
half-inch (2cm) sticks
2½ cups arborio rice

METHOD

In a large saucepan, pour in the vegetable stock and bring to the boil. Once it starts to bubble, remove from heat and set it aside.

In a new saucepan, heat the oil and add the onion and garlic. Sauté for 1-2 minutes, until they soften. Add the peas and asparagus and cook for a further 5 minutes.

Add the rice and stir with peas and asparagus for 1-2 minutes, then pour a ladle of stock and stir.

Place lid over saucepan and let rice cook until most of the stock has been absorbed. Add another ladle. Continue this step until the rice has been cooked through. Remove from heat.

Add to plates and serve.

LEAK & POTATO SOUP

PREPARATION: 15 minutes **BAKE:** 15 minutes **COOK:** 40 minutes **SERVES:** 6

INGREDIENTS

2 tbsp olive oil
1 brown onion, chopped
2 cloves of garlic, minced
3 medium-size leeks
6 medium-sized potatoes, cut into cubes
2 vegan stock cubes
1½ litres water
400g light coconut milk

Croutons:
6 slices of bread
3 tbsp olive oil
2 tsp salt
1 tsp onion powder
1 tsp garlic powder
½ tsp ground pepper

METHOD

In a medium saucepan, add the olive oil, onion and garlic and cook until onion and garlic soften.

Add the leeks and cook until leaks begin to sweat. Around 10-15 minutes. Add the potatoes and sauté for a further 5 minutes.

When the potatoes begin to turn semi-translucent, add the stock cubes and water.

Bring to the boil, then simmer for 25-30 minutes until the potatoes become soft. Add more water if the soup looked too dry. Cool for 15 minutes before blending soup to form a thick liquid.

While the soup cools, make the croutons. First, take the cubed bread and lay it on a baking tray lined with baking paper. Drizzle with oil, salt, onion powder, garlic powder and pepper and toss to combine. Bake in the oven for 15 minutes or until bread is crusty.

Take the saucepan of soup and place it back on the stove. Add the coconut cream, stir and bring to the boil. Simmer for another 5 minutes, then remove from heat. Add salt and pepper to taste.

TOMATO & PEAS ARANCINI

PREPARATION: 40 minutes   **COOK:** 55 minutes   **SERVES:** 8

INGREDIENTS

1 tbsp olive oil
1 onion
2 garlic cloves
1 cup frozen peas
1 litre tomato passata
sauce
½ tsp sugar
1 tsp salt
2 cups rice
100g vegan mozzarella
750ml vegetable oil

Arancini crust:
250g breadcrumbs
salt and pepper to taste

Arancini batter:
6 tbsp plain flour
150ml water
½ tsp salt

METHOD

In a medium saucepan, heat 1 tbsp olive oil, add the onion and garlic and sauté. Add the frozen peas and cook for 5 minutes, until peas are cooked through. Add the passata, sugar and salt and cook until thick, roughly 20 minutes.

In another saucepan, cook the rice in salted water. Drain and add ½ cup of the tomato sauce. Stir until rice is coated and set aside to cool for 10-15 minutes.

Mix the breadcrumbs, salt and pepper until combined and set aside, then make the batter by mixing the flour, water and salt until it forms a thick glue consistency.

When the rice is cool to handle, take a handful and roll it into an oval shape. Press the centre with your thumb to make a shallow well. Place a teaspoon of peas sauce and a small bunch of mozzarella, then roll rice again until it's covered. Repeat until no rice is left. Coat in batter and roll into breadcrumbs.

Preheat oil in a deep pan and add the arancini a few at a time. Cook until golden. Serve warm.

MAINS

PUMPKIN ROAST

PREPARATION: 15 minutes   **BAKE:** 1.5 hours   **COOK:** 40 minutes   **SERVES:** 8

INGREDIENTS

½ cup tri-colour quinoa
1 cups water
1 large butternut pumpkin
1 brown onion, diced
2 garlic cloves, minced
1 carrot, diced
400g can of brown lentils
2 cups baby spinach
1 tsp smoked paprika
salt and pepper, to taste
½ cup pine nuts
½ cup cranberries

METHOD

Preheat the oven to 350°F (180°C).

Cook quinoa using cooking instructions on packet. Set aside to cool.

Prepare the pumpkin by removing the top and scooping out the insides about 2 inches (5cms) in diameter. Reserve the pumpkin pieces and bake the pumpkin for 20 minutes in the oven, covering with aluminium foil.

In a large saucepan, sauté the onion and garlic until softened, then add the carrot, left over pumpkin, lentils and baby spinach. Sauté until carrots have cooked through and spinach has wilted. Add seasoning, smoked paprika, cranberries and pine nuts and continue cooking for another 5 minutes. Remove from heat.

Add the quinoa to the lentil mixture and mix well. Spoon this into the roast pumpkin and replace the "lid". Return to oven and bake with aluminium for 1 hour. Remove aluminium and continue baking until the skin of the pumpkin begins to blister (roughly 30 minutes).

Serve warm.

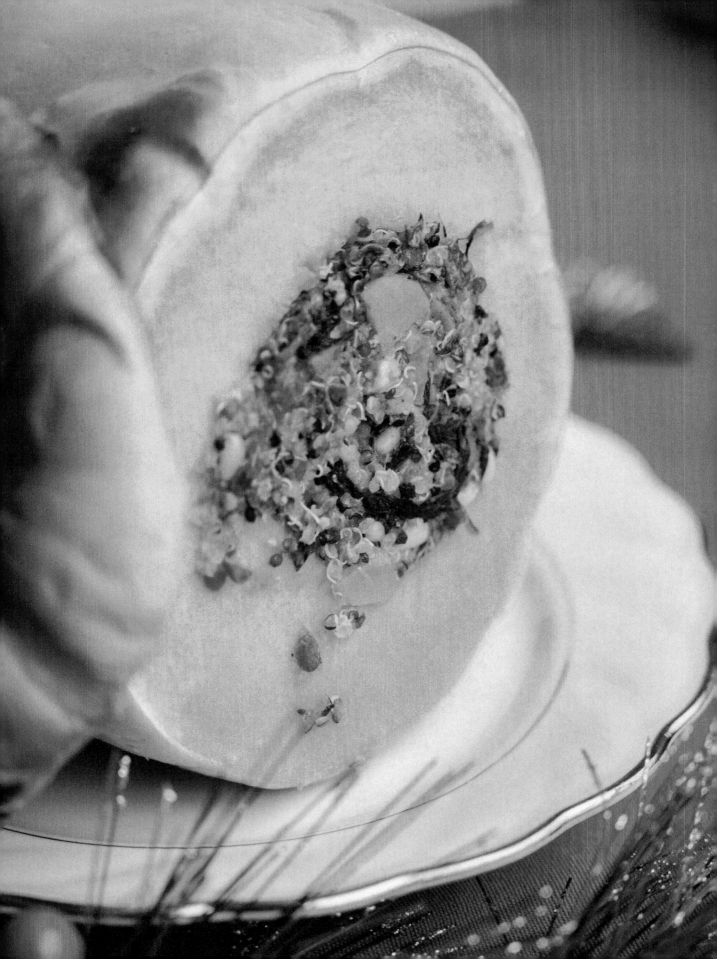

TOFU & VEGIE SKEWERS

PREPARATION: 30 minutes   **COOK:** 10 minutes   **SERVES:** 6

INGREDIENTS

450g firm tofu, drained
and pressed to release
moisture
1 red pepper, cut into
squares
1 yellow pepper, cut into
squares
1 red onion, cut into
large chunks
100g cherry tomatoes
1 zucchini (courgette),
thickly sliced

Marinade:
¼ cup dark soy sauce
¼ cup soy sauce

METHOD

Pour the soy sauces into a deep plate and add the tofu, coating evenly. Set aside to marinate for a minimum of 30 minutes

Prepare skewers by wetting them with water, then slide the vegetables and tofu, alternating between them. Leave about half an inch (1-2cms) on both sides of the skewer.

Heat a grilling pan on the stove and when it's ready to cook, place the skewers in and drizzle over the remaining marinade.

Cook evenly on all sides for 2-3 minutes, until vegetables and tofu colour and caramelise.

Serving Suggestion: Serve with a fresh green salad or steamed rice.

SWEET POTATO WELLINGTON

PREPARATION: 15 minutes   **BAKE:** 55 minutes   **COOK:** 15 minutes   **SERVES:** 8

INGREDIENTS

1 large sweet potato,
peeled and halved
length-ways
1 tbsp olive oil
1 brown onion, diced
2 garlic cloves, minced
2 cups baby spinach
400g white cup or
portobello mushrooms,
diced into small pieces
1 tsp dried thyme
1 tsp salt
½ tsp ground black
pepper
1 sheet vegan puff pastry
50g vegan feta,
crumbled
1 tbsp soy milk

METHOD

Preheat the oven to 350°F (180°C).

Bake the sweet potato for 20-25 minutes, until soft, and remove from oven.

In a medium saucepan, add the olive oil, onion and garlic and cook until onion and garlic soften.

Add the spinach and mushroom and cook for 10 minutes. Add the thyme and seasoning, stir and taste. Continue adding seasoning or thyme to taste. Remove from heat and drain away any excess water.

Take the puff pastry and add spoonfuls of the mushroom mixture to one side, leaving half an inch (1.5cms) from the corners. Sprinkle with the feta cheese and add the sweet potato. Pour remaining mushroom mixture on top and add the rest of the feta. Take the opposite end of the pastry and pull it over the filling. Align it with the edge of the pastry and press down until the mushroom mixture is fully enclosed. Brush top with soy milk

Bake for 30 minutes, until pastry is golden.

ROOT VEGETABLE MINI POT PIES

PREPARATION: 10 minutes   **BAKE**: 25 minutes   **COOK**: 20 minutes   **SERVES**: 4

INGREDIENTS

2 tbsp olive oil
1 brown onion, diced
2 garlic cloves, minced
1 tsp salt
½ tsp pepper
1 tsp dried thyme
1 leak, sliced
1 large potato, cut into
half-inch chunks
2 carrots, sliced
1 small sweet potato, cut
into half-inch chunks
1 celery, sliced
¼ butternut pumpkin,
cut into half-inch
chunks
½ cup vegetable stock
1 tbsp corn flour
1 sheets vegan puff
pastry, thawed

METHOD

Preheat the oven to 350°F (180°C).

Heat the oil in a large saucepan and sauté the onion and garlic. Add the vegetables, seasoning and thyme and cook until they soften (about 5 minutes). Add vegetable stock, cover and bring to the boil. Lower the heat and simmer for 10 minutes. Add the cornflour and stir. Continue cooking until liquid thickens. Remove from heat.

Pour into ramekins, leaving a little space from the brim.

Cut the puff pastry into quarters and place each quarter on top of a ramekin. Press the pastry into the edges.

Place into over and bake until the pastry tops turn golden, around 25 minutes.

Serve warm.

MEXICAN BAKED PEPPERS

PREPARATION: 15 minutes **BAKE:** 15 minutes **COOK:** 25 minutes **SERVES:** 8

INGREDIENTS

2 tbsp olive oil
1 brown onion, diced
2 garlic cloves, minced
140g tomato paste
1½ cups white rice
1 litre vegetable stock
½ tbsp Mexican spice mix
1 red pepper, diced
1 cup frozen corn
1 cup frozen peas
400g can black beans
1 tsp salt
½ tsp pepper
8 red peppers, cored and seeds
½ cup vegan shredded cheese

METHOD

In a medium saucepan, add the olive oil, onion and garlic and cook until onion and garlic soften. Add the tomato paste and rice and cook for an extra 4-5 minutes. Pour in ¾ of the vegetable stock and cover, bringing it to the boil before lowering the heat. Leave to simmer for 15 minutes, until the rice is almost cooked through.

Add the Mexican spice mix, remaining stock, diced peppers, corn, peas and black beans. Cook for another 3-4 minutes, until the vegetables have cooked and add salt and pepper. Stir and remove from heat.

Parboil the peppers in boiling salted water for 10 minutes before carefully removing them and place them on an oven tray with opening facing up. While you wait for peppers to cook, preheat the oven to 350°F (180°C).

Add the shredded cheese to the rice mixture and stir until combined. Add spoonfuls of the rice to each pepper. Bake for 15 minutes, until the skin of the peppers start to blister.

Remove from oven and serve.

SIDES

CUCUMBER AND TOMATO SALAD

PREPARATION: 10 minutes   **COOK:** 0 minutes   **SERVES:** 6

INGREDIENTS

5 tomatoes, cut into
wedges
1 large cucumber,
thickly sliced
1 red onion, thickly
sliced
¼ cup extra virgin olive
oil
1 heaped tsp oregano
½ tsp salt

METHOD

In a salad bowl, add the tomatoes, cucumber and
onion. Mix to combine.

Add the oregano and salt.

When ready to serve, pour over the extra virgin
olive oil.

**NOTE: Only pour the oil when serving this
salad, as oil will cause tomatoes and cucumbers
to soften once left out for a while.**

LEMON & HERB ROAST POTATOES

PREPARATION: 10 minutes **BAKE:** 45 minutes **COOK:** 10 minutes **SERVES:** 8

INGREDIENTS

6 large white potatoes, peeled and cut into large cubes
3 tbsp olive oil
1 tsp salt
½ tsp black pepper
juice from 2 lemons
vest from 2 lemons
1 tsp mixed herbs mix

METHOD

Preheat the oven to 350°F (180°C).

In a medium saucepan, parboil the potatoes in salted water for 10 minutes. Drain and return to the saucepan.

Place lid on top and give the potatoes a rough toss for a few seconds, to fluff up the edges (this will allow potatoes to crisp up in the oven).

Place potatoes on a large oven tray and add oil, salt, pepper, lemon juice and zest and mixed herbs. Mix well using your hands so each potato is coated.

Transfer to the oven and bake for 45 minutes, turning halfway, until potatoes are golden and crisp and a fork can be inserted into potatoes easily.

Serve warm.

MASHED POTATO

PREPARATION: 10 minutes   **COOK: 25** minutes   **SERVES:** 6

INGREDIENTS

6 medium russet
potatoes, cut into large
cubes
4-5 tbsp vegan butter
1 tsp salt
½ tsp black pepper

METHOD

In a medium saucepan, boil the potatoes in salted water until soft (15-20 minutes).

Drain potatoes and mash them using a potato masher.

Place mashed potatoes on the stove on low heat and add butter, salt and pepper. Stir through until ingredients are mixed well.

Pour into a serving plate and sprinkle some pepper or top with a little extra vegan butter.

ROCKET, PEAR & WALNUT SALAD

PREPARATION: 10 minutes   **COOK:** 0 minutes   **SERVES:** 6

INGREDIENTS

200g baby rocket
2 Beurre Bosc pears, cut
into thin slices
½ cup walnuts, roughly
crumbled

Dressing:
¼ cup olive oil
2 tbsp balsamic vinegar

METHOD

Add baby rocket, pears and walnuts into a salad bowl.

Mix olive oil and balsamic in a small bowl until combined and pour over the salad.

Serve immediately.

COUSCOUS SALAD

PREPARATION: 15 minutes   **COOK:** 6 minutes   **SERVES:** 6

INGREDIENTS

1 cup couscous
1⅓ cups boiling water
1 large cucumber, cubed
1 small red onion, cubed
250g cherry tomatoes,
cut in half
½ cup parsley, chopped
1 small red pepper,
cubed
1 small yellow pepper,
cubed
¼ cup Kalamata olives,
pitted and sliced

Dressing:
1 tbsp extra virgin olive
oil
1 tbsp balsamic vinegar
½ tsp salt
¼ tsp pepper
½ tsp onion powder
½ tsp garlic powder
½ tsp dried oregano

METHOD

In a medium-sized bowl, add the couscous and cover with boiling water. Let it sit for 6 minutes, then take a fork and give it a stir to fluff it up. (Please note, some couscous might need to be prepared using another method. Check your pack for instructions).

When the couscous has cooled, add the vegetables and stir through.

To make the dressing, place all ingredients into a small bowl and mix until well combined. Pour over the couscous salad, mix and serve.

DESSERTS

CHOC. COCONUT RUM BALLS

PREPARATION: 15 minutes   **REFRIGERATE:** 4 hours   **SERVES:** 8

INGREDIENTS

250g plain sweet
biscuits, crushed
1 cup shredded coconut
320g can coconut
condensed milk
¼ cup cocoa powder
1-2 tbsp rum (optional)

Ganache:
⅓ cup coconut oil,
melted
⅓ cup maple syrup
⅓ cup cacao powder

METHOD

Mix biscuits, shredded coconut, coconut condensed milk, cocoa powder and rum until all combined.

Roll into small balls, roughly the size of standard chocolate truffles. Place in the fridge to set for four hours.

To make vegan ganache, mix the coconut oil, maple syrup and cacao powder until well combined.

Take the rum balls out of the fridge and drizzle with ganache. Add your sprinkles of choice.

Store in fridge until ready to serve.

NOTE: Ganache will harden within minutes, so make sure your sprinkles are at hand to top immediately.

CHOC. HAZELNUT CHRISTMAS TREE

PREPARATION: 5 minutes   **BAKE: 25** minutes   **SERVES**: 6

INGREDIENTS

2 vegan puff pastry
sheets, thawed
¾ cup vegan chocolate
hazelnut spread
1 tbsp soy milk

METHOD

Preheat the oven to 350°F (180°C).

Take pastry sheets and cut them into identical triangles by carving a line from the middle of the top of the pastry out to each bottom edge. Remove excess pastry and place onto an oven tray lined with baking paper.

Spread chocolate hazelnut spread over one layer of pastry and top with the second sheet.

Carve equal lines from each side going into the middle of the pastry, making sure to stop about an inch from the middle on either side.

Gently twist the sides of each pastry flap you have created. Brush some soy milk over the top of the pastry and place into the oven.

Bake for 20-25 minutes, until pastry is golden.

SHORTBREAD COOKIES

PREPARATION: 20 minutes   **BAKE:** 15 minutes   **SERVES:** 8

INGREDIENTS

250g vegan butter, softened
½ cup caster sugar
1 tsp vanilla extract
1¾ cups plain flour
⅔ cup rice flour
½ tsp salt

METHOD

Preheat the oven to 350°F (180°C) and line 2 oven trays with baking paper.

Beat the butter and sugar in a mixing bowl until creamy, then add the vanilla and stir through.

Add the flours and salt and mix until dough comes together. Knead in the bowl for a minute, then cover in plastic wrap and place in fridge for 30 minutes to rest.

Transfer to a lightly floured surface and roll out the dough until it's about ⅓ inch (1cm) and use cookie cutter of choice to cut your shapes. Add cookie to baking tray, then roll the dough back into a ball and roll out again. Repeat process with cookie cutter until no dough is left.

Place cookies in the oven for 12-15 minutes, until golden.

Remove from oven and let stand for 5 minutes before transferring to a cooling rack to cool completely.

CHOCOLATE BUNDT CAKE

PREPARATION: 10 minutes   **BAKE:** 55 minutes   **SERVES:** 10

INGREDIENTS

2 tbsp ground flaxseed
6 tbsp water
2½ cups plain flour
1 cup cocoa powder
½ tsp salt
¾ cups caster sugar
¼ cup brown sugar
2 tsp baking powder
1 tsp baking soda
1 cup plant-milk
1 tsp vanilla extract
½ cup vegetable oil
1 cup hot coffee

Ganache:

⅓ cup coconut oil, melted
⅓ cup maple syrup
⅓ cup cacao powder

METHOD

Preheat the oven to 350°F (180°C) and grease a bundt pan.

In a cup, place the flaxseed and water and set aside for 5 minutes, until it becomes thick. This will be your egg substitute.

In a large mixing bowl, add the flour, cocoa powder, salt, sugars, baking powder and baking soda. Mix together, then add the flax egg, milk, vanilla extract and oil. Mix until combined.

Add the cup of coffee and mix until all are combined. Pour into the bundt pan.

Bake in the oven for 55 minutes to 1 hour, until a wooden skewer can be inserted and come back out clean. Remove from oven and set aside for 10 minutes before transferring to a cooling rack.

Make vegan ganache by mixing the coconut oil, maple syrup and cacao powder until well combined. Pour over the top of the bundt cake once it has cooled down completely. Serve as is or with a dusting of icing sugar on top.

COOKIES & CREAM TRUFFLES

PREPARATION: 15 minutes + 1 hour   **REFRIGERATE:** 4 hours   **SERVES:** 8

INGREDIENTS

250g chocolate and
cream biscuits
150g vegan cream cheese

Ganache:
⅓ cup coconut oil,
melted
⅓ cup maple syrup
⅓ cup cacao powder

METHOD

Process the chocolate and cream biscuits in a food processor until they form a crumbed texture.

Pour crumbled biscuits to a mixing bowl and add the vegan cream cheese. Mix to combine.

Roll into equal balls the size of a small walnut and place into the fridge to set for an hour.

In the meantime, make the ganache by mixing the coconut oil, maple syrup and cacao powder together until it forms a thick liquid. This will harden at room temperature and may need to be microwaved for a few seconds to remain smooth and runny.

When the truffles are firm, remove them from the fridge and roll them gently into the ganache using a fork. Place them on a tray lined with baking paper and add any decorations you want while the ganache is still runny.

Return to the fridge to set completely for another hour.

DRINKS

COCONUT HOT CHOCOLATE

PREPARATION: 2 minutes   **COOK:** 5 minutes   **SERVES:** 2

INGREDIENTS

2 cup coconut milk
1 tbsp cacao powder
½ tsp coconut essence
(optional)
¼ cup shredded coconut

METHOD

Place coconut milk in a small saucepan on the stove and heat for several minutes until milk is hot, but not boiling.

Add cacao powder, shredded coconut and coconut essence and stir until well combined.

Once the surface of the milk mixture starts to thicken and a light froth appears, remove from heat and serve.

VEGAN EGGNOG

PREPARATION: 15 minutes   **COOK:** 6 minutes   **SERVES:** 2

INGREDIENTS

1 cup cashews, soaked overnight
2 cups plant-based milk of choice
¼ tsp ground cinnamon
¼ tsp ground nutmeg
3 tbsp maple syrup
½ tsp vanilla extract
¼ tsp ground clove
1-2 tbsp rum or bourbon (optional)

METHOD

Add the cashews, milk, spices, vanilla extract and maple syrup to a high-speed blender and blend until smooth.

Add rum or bourbon and mix together.

Serve cold, at room temperature or warm with a dusting of cinnamon on top.

GINGERBREAD HOT CHOCOLATE

PREPARATION: 2 minutes   **COOK:** 5 minutes   **SERVES:** 2

INGREDIENTS

2 cups plant milk of choice
2 tbsp cocoa powder
½ tsp cinnamon
¼ tsp ground ginger
¼ tsp allspice
½ tsp vanilla extract
2 tbsp maple syrup

METHOD

Pour plant milk into a small saucepan and heat until warm.

Add remaining ingredients and stir until combined.

Simmer for 5 minutes, stirring occasionally.

Pour into mugs and add your toppings of choice.

PINK SANGRIA

PREPARATION: 10 minutes   **COOK:** 0 minutes   **SERVES:** 6

INGREDIENTS

750ml pink Moscato
750ml white Moscato
¼ cup brandy
500ml lemonade
1 punnet strawberries,
sliced
2 peaches, peeled and
cubed
1 orange, cubed
1 apple, cubed
1 cup ice
1 bunch mint leaves
(optional)

METHOD

In a large jug, pour in wines, brandy and lemonade. Chill for several hours, or overnight for best results.

Add the strawberries, peaches, orange and apple to the wine mixture, stirring to combine.

Once ready to serve, add the ice and mint leaves.

CRANBERRY & LIME SPARKLER

PREPARATION: 3 minutes   **COOK:** 0 minutes   **SERVES:** 6

INGREDIENTS

750ml cranberry juice
500ml sparkling mineral
water
1 lime, halved and cut
into slices
3 cups ice

METHOD

In a large jug, add the cranberry juice and
sparkling water.

Add half a cup of ice to a glass and 3-4 lime
slices.

Pour over cranberry drink and serve
immediately.

DISCLAIMER:

All opinions and recommendations contained in this book are those of the author and are not substitutes for professional advice or medical treatment. Any reader with a medical condition, or suspected medical condition, should seek professional medical advice from their doctor. The author or publisher will not be held liable from any action or claim resulting from the use of this book or any information contained herein.

Printed in Great Britain
by Amazon